W9-BLK-421

The Japanese American Internment

PERSPECTIVES ON

The Japanese American Internment

Innocence, Guilt, and Wartime Justice

ANN HEINRICHS

mc **Marshall Cavendish**
Benchmark
New York

Published by Marshall Cavendish Benchmark
An imprint of Marshall Cavendish Corporation

Other Marshall Cavendish Offices: Marshall Cavendish International (Asia) Private Limited, 1 New Industrial Road, Singapore 536196 • Marshall Cavendish International (Thailand) Co Ltd. 253 Asoke, 12th Flr, Sukhumvit 21 Road, Klongtoey Nua, Wattana, Bangkok 10110, Thailand • Marshall Cavendish (Malaysia) Sdn Bhd, Times Subang, Lot 46, Subang Hi-Tech Industrial Park, Batu Tiga, 40000 Shah Alam, Selangor Darul Ehsan, Malaysia

Marshall Cavendish is a trademark of Times Publishing Limited

All websites were available and accurate when this book was sent to press.

Library of Congress Cataloging-in-Publication Data

Heinrichs, Ann.
The Japanese American internment : innocence, guilt, and wartime justice / by Ann Heinrichs.
p. cm. — (Perspectives on)
Summary: "Provides comprehensive information on the Japanese American internment in the United States and the differing perspectives accompanying it"—Provided by publisher.
Includes bibliographical references and index.
ISBN 978-0-7614-4983-6
1. Japanese Americans—Evacuation and relocation, 1942–1945—Juvenile literature. 2. World War, 1939–1945—Japanese Americans—Juvenile literature. 3. Japanese—United States—History—Juvenile literature. I. Title.
D769.8.A6H45 2011
940.53'1773—dc22
2009035467

Editor: Christine Florie
Publisher: Michelle Bisson
Art Director: Anahid Hamparian
Series Designer: Sonia Chaghatzbanian

Expert reader: Daryl J. Maeda, Assistant professor of ethnic studies,
University of Colorado at Boulder

Photo research by Marybeth Kavanagh

Cover photo by Apic/Getty Images

The photographs in this book are used by permission and through the courtesy of:
Getty Images: Eliot Elisofon/Time & Life Pictures, 2–3; Dorothea Lange, 13, 23; Keystone, 15, 20, 27; Russell Lee, 39; Buyenlarge, 49; David McNew/Newsmakers, 74; Bachrach, 76L; Pictorial Parade, 76R; *The Granger Collection*: 8, 31; *Alamy*: North Wind Picture Archives, 10; *The Art Archive*: National Archives Washington, DC, 16; *Corbis*: 36, 51; Bettmann, 50, 61; Wally McNamee, 71; *AP Photo*: 44, 46, 65; Barry Thumma, 67; National Park Service, 82; *The Image Works*: Larry Mulvehill, 78

Printed in Malaysia (T)
1 3 5 6 4 2

Contents

Introduction

IT WAS A SCENE NEVER BEFORE WITNESSED in the nation's history. More than 110,000 U.S. residents — men, women, and children of Japanese ancestry — were rounded up under military guard and sent to desolate camps surrounded by barbed wire fences. There they were interned, or imprisoned, from 1942 to 1945. These camps have variously been called relocation centers, internment camps, and concentration camps.

The Japanese American internment occurred at a time when fears about national security were running high. World War II (1939–1945) was in full force, with the United States at war both in Europe and in the Pacific region. As Japan was the major adversary in the Pacific, Japanese Americans along the Pacific coast were viewed with suspicion. Did their loyalties lie with Japan, many Americans wondered, or with the United States? The U.S. government decided that, for purposes of national security, people of Japanese ancestry should be confined under heavy guard until Japan was no longer a threat.

No citizens voted on the internment. Neither did their representatives in Congress, although Congress lent support to the measure. Instead, it was the result of a wartime proclamation issued by President Franklin D. Roosevelt.

Still, public opinion largely supported the move, or at least accepted it as a wartime precaution. As a backdrop to these sentiments, Japanese Americans had been targets of racial prejudice for decades.

The Japanese American internment raises some tough questions. Who was responsible for it, and how did it come about? Was it a necessary act of wartime, the result of wartime panic, or the culmination of longstanding ethnic prejudice? How could other Americans, themselves the descendants of immigrant communities, stand by and watch this happen? Was the government justified in using ethnic identity as a reason for depriving people of their constitutionally guaranteed freedoms? If not, how are we making sure this does not happen again? And what have we learned from this episode in U.S. history?

These questions remain vitally important today, more than sixty years later. To consider them, we must explore the social, economic, and political context of the internment and the events leading up to it. Once we have examined the perspectives and motivations of all parties, we can begin to understand the emotions and thought processes that brought about this incident. Using what we learn, we can approach similar circumstances more wisely as we reach toward the ideal of liberty and justice for all.

Note: Some terms used in this text conform to the traditional terminology that conveys the government's perspective at the time. However, terms like *evacuation, relocation, evacuee,* and *assembly center* tend to obscure the facts and minimize the seriousness of the internment. Other words in this text, such as *internment, detention, imprison,* and *internee,* reflect a more balanced perspective gained with hindsight.

One

A Swelling
Tide of
Suspicion

ANTI-JAPANESE SENTIMENT HAD ITS ROOTS in United States soil in the late 1800s, when the first wave of Japanese laborers arrived. Already, Americans on the West Coast were prejudiced against Chinese people. Thousands of Chinese laborers had been brought in to help build the transcontinental railroad, completed in 1869. Those workers went on to open businesses or labor on farms. Because the Chinese were willing to work for low wages, Caucasians resented them, saying that they were taking jobs away from native-born Americans. Anti-Chinese labor leaders, politicians, and citizens' groups in California began to push for more restrictions against Chinese people. Eventually, in 1882, Congress passed the Chinese Exclusion Act, barring further Chinese immigration. That created a labor shortage and a need to find another source of low-wage workers.

Beginning in 1885 planters recruited Japanese farm workers to labor on Hawaii's sugar plantations and California's fruit and vegetable farms. The criteria for selection included expertise in agriculture and a solid work ethic.

In 1882 Congress prohibited Chinese immigration by passing the Chinese Exclusion Act. This political cartoon created at the time satirizes the act.

By 1890 there were 2,038 Japanese people in the United States. Thousands more continued to arrive. Many took up crop farming or cultivated fruit-tree orchards, while others operated fishing boats, ran small retail businesses, or worked for large companies. Often whole families worked on the farms or in the shops.

Now the old anti-Chinese prejudice easily shifted to the Japanese. Both groups were seen as separate and distinct racially, standing apart from American society as a whole. Because of their Asian features and cultural traditions, they did not blend into American life as inconspicuously as immigrant groups from Europe did. In 1892 three San Francisco newspapers began publishing anti-Japanese articles. This effort led San Francisco's board of education to pass an 1893

Japanese workers cure raisins in California vineyards in 1890.

resolution that Japanese children had to attend segregated Chinese schools. After the Japanese government's representative to San Francisco protested, the board withdrew the resolution, but the prejudice remained intact.

Eventually Japanese immigrants began to lease farmland and to work as sharecroppers for Caucasian farmers. The increased presence of Japanese people in agriculture only added to anti-Japanese sentiment. In 1905 the *San Francisco Chronicle* began a campaign against Japanese Americans in California. Typical headlines were vicious and mean-spirited:

THE YELLOW PERIL — HOW JAPANESE CROWD OUT THE WHITE RACE

BROWN ARTISANS STEAL BRAINS OF WHITES

CRIME AND POVERTY GO HAND IN HAND WITH ASIATIC LABOR

JAPANESE A MENACE TO AMERICAN WOMEN

Politicians and labor leaders joined the outcry. In 1905 dozens of California labor unions formed the Asiatic Exclusion League. Its expressed aim was to spread anti-Asian propaganda and to lobby for legislation barring Asian immigrants. These tensions led to what is called the Gentlemen's Agreement, formed between the United States and Japan in 1907. It was agreed that Japan would limit emigration to the United States, and the United States would ease up on anti-Japanese discrimination. Nevertheless, both emigration and discrimination continued.

Farming was the backbone of the Japanese American economy. As Japanese farming ventures became more successful, California's Caucasian farmers pressured state legislators to pass the Alien Land Law of 1913, which barred "aliens ineligible to citizenship" from owning land.

(Aliens are foreign-born people who are not U.S. citizens.) Since the majority of Japanese Americans lived in California, this was a heavy blow to their community. Washington State, where many Japanese immigrants had settled, later passed its own Alien Land Law. Both laws were specifically aimed at the Japanese.

Meanwhile, the Seattle-based Anti-Japanese League added to the growing tide of anti-Japanese attitudes. Its members saw the Japanese as a threat to U.S. workers and pushed to bar them from operating businesses. League members, Seattle politicians, farmers, and labor leaders testified before Congress about the effects of Japanese labor. Influenced by these statements, Congress passed the Immigration Act of 1924, which cut off Japanese immigration altogether.

The Japanese American Community

Japanese Americans tended to live in all-Japanese communities (*nihonmachi*). This was because they wanted to be near relatives, as well as Japanese friends and stores. But there was another reason, as well: the racial prejudice that barred them from other areas. Residents built Christian churches and Buddhist and Shinto temples in their communities and celebrated religious and cultural festivals together. They also opened clubs devoted to recreation, civic pride, or cultural pursuits ranging from language study to traditional Japanese flower arranging. Education was valued highly. Japanese American children excelled in public schools, and many went on to colleges and universities.

There were several categories of Japanese Americans, based on generational factors. The *Issei* had been born in Japan and immigrated to the United States. The *Nisei* were their children who had been born in the United States and were U.S. citizens by birth. The *Sansei* were children of the Nisei, with immigrant grandparents. Each generation was more firmly rooted in American culture than the one before.

By 1940, 126,947 Japanese people and people of Japanese descent lived on the U.S. mainland. Of those, 88.5 percent lived on the West Coast and almost three-fourths lived in California. Other large populations lived in Washington State and Oregon. Among the 93,717 people classified as Japanese Americans living in California in 1940, 33,569

The Japanese American community designated themselves by generation. This family represents Nisei and Sansei.

were immigrant Issei and 60,148 were Nisei. In addition, 157,905 people of Japanese ancestry lived in Hawaii, which was a U.S. territory at the time.

The Outbreak of War

Throughout the 1930s, conflicts in Europe and Asia produced growing tensions worldwide. In Germany Adolf Hitler led the Nazi (or National Socialist German Workers) Party, which promoted the idea of the superiority of the German nation. Racism was a hallmark of Nazi thinking, too, with so-called Aryan (northern European) ethnic groups regarded as superior. Especially prominent in the Nazi outlook was anti-Semitism, or prejudice against Jewish people. Hitler became Germany's chancellor in 1933 and the next year was elected president as well.

Driven to gain more territory for Germany, Hitler began annexing European lands. When he invaded Poland in September 1939, other nations rallied to stop him. This marked the beginning of World War II, with the Allied powers, or Allies, pitted against Germany and the nations aligned with it, the Axis powers.

At first, the Allies consisted of Poland, Great Britain, and France. In the months to come, dozens of nations joined, including Australia, India, Canada, Norway, Belgium, Greece, and the Soviet Union. The major Axis powers would be Germany, Italy, and Japan. Among their many coalition partners were Hungary, Romania, Bulgaria, and Yugoslavia.

In Asia, meanwhile, the Japanese Empire was clashing with China and Russia and seizing Asian territories. These activities heightened the U.S. government's apprehensions

Japanese troops invade Pacific shores during World War II.

about Japan—and about Japanese Americans who might be loyal to Japan. Such fears increased even more after Japan joined the Axis powers in 1940.

Government Perspectives: National Security or Racial Prejudice?

With conflicts escalating in both Europe and Asia, national security became a growing preoccupation within the U.S. government. As Japan became ever more militant, Japanese Americans living in the far-western United States were especially suspect, as that could be an ideal location for communicating with the enemy. Some thought that Japanese Americans might commit sabotage (by destroying military

This U.S. propaganda poster is designed to stir up sentiment against allegedly disloyal Japanese Americans.

facilities along the West Coast) or espionage (by acting as spies who relayed sensitive information to Japan). Rumors circulated about the so-called fifth column, an alleged network of Japanese Americans who conspired to aid Japan.

Many government officials saw loyalty as inextricably bound with ethnic identity. As early as 1934 a U.S. State Department memo warned that "when war breaks out, the entire Japanese population on the West Coast will rise and commit sabotage." Lieutenant General John DeWitt, who oversaw the internment process, also linked ethnicity with threats to national security:

> The continued presence of a large,
> unassimilated, tightly knit and racial group,
> bound to an enemy nation by strong ties of
> race, culture, custom and religion along a
> frontier vulnerable to attack constituted
> a menace which had to be dealt with.

In 1939 as the prospect of war loomed ever closer, President Franklin Delano Roosevelt directed the Federal Bureau of Investigation (FBI) to begin assembling names of aliens with "suspicious" backgrounds or activities. Those considered to be especially dangerous would be arrested in the event of war. Among the Japanese community, the list included hundreds of prominent Issei men.

As a further national security measure, Congress passed the Alien Registration Act of 1940. It required all foreign nationals aged fourteen and up to register, be fingerprinted, and provide detailed personal information. Later the government would use this information as a tool against many Japanese Americans.

Various government agencies conducted investigations, each trying to determine how dangerous Japanese Americans might be. In July 1940 the Office of Naval Intelligence assigned Lieutenant Commander Kenneth Ringle to investigate Japanese Americans on the West Coast. Ringle found them to be unthreatening:

First, the West Coast Japanese were . . .
increasingly Americanized and, like most
immigrant groups, believed intensely in the
United States and its vision of a better life.
Second, in spite of their eagerness to be
identified as Americans and their record of
industry and responsibility, the Japanese on
the West Coast were continually subjected to
every sort of discrimination—discrimination
as brutal and mindless as anything the South
ever inflicted on the Negro.

President Roosevelt sent a U.S. State Department representative, Curtis B. Munson, to the West Coast to determine
how loyal Japanese Americans were. Munson's 1941 report,
too, seemed reassuring:

[T]here is no Japanese "problem" on the
Coast. There will be no armed uprising
of Japanese. . . . [F]or the most part the local
Japanese are loyal to the U.S. or, at worst,
hope that by remaining quiet they can avoid
concentration camps or irresponsible mobs.
We do not believe that they would be at least
any more disloyal than any other racial group
in the United States with whom we are at war.

In spite of these reports, many government officials were
blatantly prejudiced on racial grounds. Among them, in addition to DeWitt, were Secretary of War Henry L. Stimson and
President Roosevelt himself. Like many other Americans,

Roosevelt looked on the Japanese in a coolly impersonal way. He once suggested that their "skull pattern, being less developed than that of the Caucasians, might be responsible for their aggressive behavior." With such a perspective, Roosevelt was inclined to give favorable attention to his anti-Japanese advisers. Yet with World War II raging in Europe, and Japan a growing concern, the United States at first managed to stay out of the conflicts.

Pearl Harbor

American neutrality ended on December 7, 1941, when Japanese bombers attacked the U.S. Navy fleet at Pearl Harbor on the Hawaiian island of Oahu. The attack immediately changed the status of Japanese people in the United States. That same day, President Roosevelt issued Presidential Proclamation No. 2525. It declared all Japanese noncitizens to be enemy aliens, "liable to restraint." This would set the stage for the internment to come.

On December 8 Roosevelt addressed Congress with his famous "day of infamy" speech, requesting a formal declaration of war against Japan:

> Yesterday, December 7, 1941 — a date which
> will live in infamy — the United States of
> America was suddenly and deliberately
> attacked by naval and air forces of the Empire
> of Japan. . . . I ask that the Congress declare
> that since the unprovoked and dastardly
> attack by Japan on Sunday, December
> seventh, a state of war has existed between
> the United States and the Japanese Empire.

The American destroyer USS *Shaw* explodes during the Japanese attack on Pearl Harbor in 1941.

Congress approved the declaration at once, marking the formal entry of the United States into World War II. Now, from the neighborhood level up to the highest reaches of government, a question inflamed the hearts and minds of many Americans: if Japan is the enemy, are Japanese Americans enemies, too?

Two

The Aftermath of Pearl Harbor

THE INTERNMENT ORDER FOR ALL Japanese Americans came just ten weeks after the Pearl Harbor attack. During those weeks, perspectives within the U.S. government and among the American people came into sharp focus. Pearl Harbor solidified anti-Japanese attitudes that were already in place, such as racial prejudice and economic envy. Fear and suspicion escalated, too. For those with an anti-Japanese bias, it now seemed eminently possible that the Japanese military would invade the American mainland, aided by West Coast Japanese Americans. To those in power, it became obvious that these people were a national security risk and had to be placed under guard in isolated places.

"We Wanted to Do What Was American"

Japanese Americans were just as shocked as any other Americans when they heard of the attack on Pearl Harbor. Many, like Lili Sasaki, were horrified. "I was walking home from helping my brother-in-law in his snack shop," she recalls, "and I saw the newspaper on the stand: 'Japan bombed Pearl Harbor.' Oh, I felt terrible. My god, don't tell me such an awful thing like that!" Others did not even understand the news. Hiro Mizushima wrote, "I turned on the radio and I heard about Pearl Harbor. I didn't know where Pearl Harbor was or anything."

Japanese Americans nervously watched the events after Pearl Harbor unfold. Mary Tsukamoto of Florin, California, voiced the feelings of many at the time:

> We were frightened, but . . . we frantically
> wanted to do what was American. We were
> Americans and loyal citizens, and we wanted
> to do what Americans should be doing. So
> we were wrapping Red Cross bandages
> and trying to do what we could to help our
> country. . . . We started to buy war bonds,
> and we took first aid classes with the rest of
> the [Caucasian] people in the community.

The Japanese American Citizens League (JACL) was a strong pro-American voice in the Japanese American community. Its members were Nisei. Eager to prove their loyalty, they tried hard to assure the U.S. government that they understood the need for evacuation, the first step in carrying out the internment order, and would cooperate in any way. Mike Masaoka was the JACL's national secretary during the early 1940s. He put himself forward as the official public spokesman for Japanese Americans. Masaoka testified before Congress that Japanese Americans would cooperate with any evacuation orders. Masaoka also composed a Japanese American Creed, a testimony of loyalty to the United States.

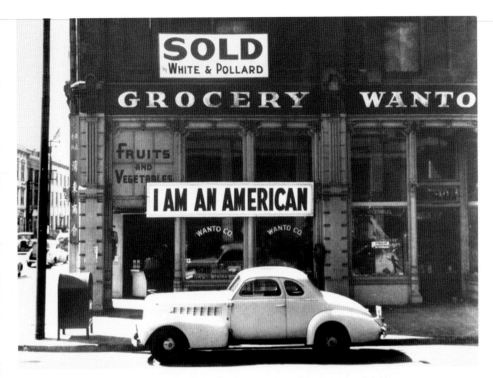

The day after the Pearl Harbor attack, a grocery store owner of Japanese descent placed this "I Am an American" sign on his storefront window. Following the evacuation orders, a "Sold" sign appeared on the building.

Many Japanese Americans disagreed with Masaoka, and not all were Issei. Many Nisei believed that this man of their generation had hijacked the voice of Japanese Americans and crowded out the true feelings of part of the community. Some even accused Masaoka of informing on those who might be disloyal, causing them to be arrested. Denver journalist and newspaper editor James Omura testified before Congress in 1942 in opposition to Masaoka's viewpoint. "I am strongly opposed to mass evacuation of American-born Japanese,"

The Japanese American Creed

Mike Masaoka called for all JACL members to embrace this creed as proof of their loyalty. Here are some excerpts:

I am proud that I am an American citizen of Japanese ancestry, [and I appreciate] the wonderful advantages of this Nation. I believe in her institutions, ideals, and traditions; I glory in her heritage; I boast of her history; I trust in her future. . . .

Although some individuals may discriminate against me, I shall never become bitter or lose faith. . . .

Because I believe in America and I trust she believes in me . . . I pledge myself to do honor to her at all times and in all places; to support her constitution; to obey her laws; to respect her flag; to defend her against all enemies, . . . in the hope that I may become a better American in a greater America.

To many Issei, Masaoka's creed went too far. They believed he was going overboard in reaching out to the U.S. government.

he said. "I have felt that the leaders [of the JACL] were leading the American-born Japanese along the wrong channels." This conflict of opinion would flare up many times in the months and years to come.

Enemy Aliens

After the Pearl Harbor attack, the Issei were declared enemy aliens. As such, they were forbidden to own contraband, or materials considered threatening to national security. Among the forbidden items were firearms, knives, short-wave radios, cameras, and "Papers, documents or books in which there may be invisible writing." Curfews were imposed, and travel and financial transactions were restricted.

"When I heard the news of Pearl Harbor," recalls Jack Matsuoka, a California teenager at the time, "I didn't believe it. My folks didn't believe it either. It never hit us until the army put out a curfew." Barry Sakai, a student at the University of California at Berkeley, was shocked as well: "The attack had suddenly changed our parents into enemy aliens. . . . Overnight, we found that we could not cash checks, as our parents' accounts were frozen under government orders."

In addition to the general alien orders, the FBI had compiled lists of Issei men they believed were especially dangerous. Among them were diplomats, professors, community leaders, business executives, bankers, newspaper editors, religious leaders, martial-arts instructors, and Japanese-language teachers. These men were quickly seized and imprisoned.

On the day of the Pearl Harbor attack, Yoshiko Uchida's father, a businessman, said the bombing was probably the

Japanese aliens from California who are considered potential threats are gathered and taken into custody in 1942.

work of some crazy fanatic. Sure that there was nothing to worry about, Yoshiko went on to the library to study. "When I got home," she said, "the house was filled with an uneasy quiet. A strange man sat in our living room and my father was gone. The FBI had come to pick him up." By December 9, two days after the attack, more than 1,200 Issei were in FBI custody. Most were shipped to a prison camp for enemy aliens in Missoula, Montana.

Public Opinion: Caucasians' Perspectives

For the most part, public opinion after Pearl Harbor followed an anti-Japanese track. Most non-Japanese Americans felt that Japan was the nation's biggest threat. In an opinion poll conducted in early 1942, two-thirds of Americans wanted President Roosevelt to direct U.S. armed forces against Japan before taking up the fight in Europe. For many Americans, hostility toward Japan seamlessly spilled over into hostility toward Japanese Americans.

Newspapers helped fan the flames of anti-Japanese American attitudes. Popular newspaper columnist Walter Lippmann of the *New York Herald-Tribune* was an influential voice. He favored evacuating Japanese Americans, saying that the West Coast was a combat zone and "nobody ought to be on a battlefield who has not good reason for being there."

For farmers, fishermen, and labor organizations, Pearl Harbor created a handy excuse to remove Japanese Americans from the West Coast. Farmers' groups pushed hard for the evacuation. By 1940 Japanese Americans were producing 10 percent of the value of California's farm products. Non-Japanese farmers wanted to get rid of the competition and snap up more valuable farmland. Austin Anson, managing secretary of the Salinas [California] Vegetable Grower-Shipper Association, was not shy about expressing his opinion. He also had no qualms about using the derogatory racial epithet "Japs"—a brisk, one-syllable way to dehumanize Japanese Americans at the time.

> We're charged with wanting to get rid of
> the Japs for selfish reasons. They came
> into this valley to work, and they stayed to

take over. . . . If all the Japs were removed tomorrow, we'd never miss them in two weeks, because the white farmers can take over and produce everything the Jap grows. And we don't want them back when the war ends, either.

Public opinion also played itself out on the grassroots, neighborhood level. For example, Japanese Americans were given an 8:00 PM curfew, but they were sometimes out later than that. According to Mary Tsukamoto, "[Caucasian] neighbors were watching us and reporting to the FBI that we were having secret meetings. . . . We would be reported, and the police would come."

Warring Perspectives within the Government

In the weeks after Pearl Harbor, the debate heated up within Roosevelt's administration about whether Japanese Americans were a threat to national security and needed to be removed. According to the FBI, there was no need to round up the entire Japanese American population on the West Coast. FBI director J. Edgar Hoover believed that the Issei his federal agents had already arrested were the only potential dangers. He wrote in a memo dated February 2, 1942:

The necessity for mass evacuation is based primarily upon public and political pressure rather than on factual data. Public hysteria and in some instances, the comments of the press and radio announcers, have resulted in a tremendous amount of pressure.

Attorney General Francis Biddle saw things the same way. He advised President Roosevelt that

> A great many West Coast people distrust the Japanese, various special interests would welcome their removal from good farm land and the elimination of their competition. . . . My last advice from the War Department is that there is no evidence of imminent attack and from the F.B.I. that there is no evidence of planned sabotage.

Still, Roosevelt had his own personal views about the danger posed by people of Japanese ancestry. Thus he was more inclined to accept the view of Lieutenant General DeWitt. DeWitt admitted that no Japanese Americans had ever committed sabotage. Nevertheless, on February 14, 1942, he issued a report recommending internment on racial grounds:

> The Japanese race is an enemy race and while many second and third generation Japanese born on United State soil, possessed of United States citizenship, have become "Americanized," the racial strains are undiluted. . . . [A]long the vital Pacific Coast over 112,000 potential enemies, of Japanese extraction, are at large today. There are indications that these were organized and ready for concerted action at a favorable opportunity. The very fact that no sabotage has taken place to date is a disturbing and confirming indication that such action will be taken.

DeWitt freely admitted that he had no way to figure out which Japanese Americans were a threat. The best solution, he concluded, was to consider everyone disloyal.

While it is believed that some were loyal, it was known that many were not. It was impossible to establish the identity of the loyal and the disloyal with any degree of safety. . . . [I] had no alternative but to

Theodor Geisel, better known as Dr. Seuss, created this political cartoon in 1942. It reflects the fear of many Americans at that time, who believed Japanese Americans were potential saboteurs in sympathy with Japan during World War II.

The Tolan Committee Hearings

After Executive Order 9066, Congress formed the Tolan Committee to solicit opinions from West Coast residents, politicians, and community leaders about the evacuation. This was largely an empty gesture, as a decision had already been made. The American Civil Liberties Union (ACLU), a civil rights organization, had legal objections. ACLU attorney A. L. Wirin testified: "We feel that treating persons, because they are members of a race, constitutes illegal discrimination, which is forbidden by the Fourteenth Amendment whether we are at war or peace."

Legal rights were of no interest to members of Portland's American Legion, a patriotic organization whose members are veterans: "[T]his is no time for namby-pamby pussyfooting, fear of hurting the feelings of our enemies; [or] consideration of minute constitutional rights of those enemies . . . it is time for . . . the removal of all enemy aliens."

Self-interest underlay the testimony of California Attorney General Earl Warren (later chief justice of the United States), who was facing reelection. Knowing that an anti-Japanese position would be popular, he raised the sabotage scare: "[T]he Japanese population of California is . . . ideally situated . . . to carry into execution a tremendous program of sabotage on a mass scale."

In the face of such input, the Tolan Committee ended up supporting the evacuation.

conclude that the Japanese constituted
a potentially dangerous element from
the viewpoint of military security—that
military necessity required their immediate
evacuation to the interior.

Thus the decision was made to remove all Japanese Americans from the West Coast. On February 19, 1942, Roosevelt issued Executive Order 9066. It declared that "war requires every possible protection against espionage and against sabotage." Therefore, the Secretary of War was authorized to designate areas "from which any or all persons may be excluded." In other words, the military could "exclude" anyone from anywhere in the United States because the country was at war. Although the term "Japanese" never appears in the order, this order set the stage for the mass evacuation of more than 110,000 Japanese Americans from their homes.

Three

Roundup and Relocation

THE "EXCLUSION ZONES," OR AREAS from which Japanese Americans would be excluded, reached from Oregon and Washington State through California and into southern Arizona. Beginning in March 1942 Japanese Americans in these zones were uprooted from their residences and eventually shipped to ten camps in remote locations away from the coast.

The "Greatest Forced Migration" Begins

The first step in the roundup came on March 2, 1942, when General DeWitt issued Public Proclamation No. 1. It announced the first exclusion zones as areas that would eventually be evacuated. The next day the *San Francisco News* reported: "Japanese on West Coast Face Wholesale Uprooting. The greatest forced migration in American history was getting under way today."

At first the government figured that Japanese Americans would voluntarily leave the coast after the exclusion zones were announced, and only a few thousand would need to be forced out. Around eight thousand people actually did move. But the great majority either could not afford the move, were confused by the orders, or feared hostility from inland communities.

By late March it was clear that relatively few people were moving on their own. The holdouts would have to be ordered to leave. On March 24, 1942, General DeWitt issued Civilian Exclusion Order No. 1. It ordered the evacuation of Japanese Americans on Bainbridge Island, Washington. Then, in one West Coast city after another, notices appeared on telephone poles and walls all over town with "Instructions to All Persons of Japanese Ancestry."

Civilian Exclusion Order No. 1 required the evacuation of Japanese living on Bainbridge Island, Washington, in March 1942. Here a military police officer posts the order.

Who Were the Evacuees?

The evacuation orders applied to anyone who was at least one-sixteenth Japanese. That meant anyone who had a single Japanese great-great-grandparent. In effect, this included anyone in the United States with any Japanese ancestry whatsoever.

About one-third of the evacuees were Issei, or Japanese immigrants, many of whom were elderly. The other two-thirds were American-born citizens. They ranged from adults and teenagers down to children and infants. Most were Nisei, many of whom also had children of their own, the Sansei.

The evacuees also included Japanese American children who had been adopted by Caucasians, children from orphanages, newborns, disabled people, and the elderly. It is estimated that more than 17,000 of the evacuees were under ten years old, and about 2,000 were over sixty-five years of age.

Families were given a week, or sometimes less, to get rid of their farms, shops, homes, and personal property by either selling or leaving behind valued and valuable possessions. Each person could bring only what he or she could carry in one bag. Pets were not permitted, and many a child said tearful good-byes to a beloved cat or dog.

Selling Out Fast: Buyers' and Sellers' Perspectives

With only a few days' notice, people had to prepare quickly. Children and teenagers quit school at once, and adults walked off their jobs. Many family farms were sold for a tiny fraction of their value. Some of the buyers were individual farmers, while others were large corporations. According to agriculture activist A. V. Krebs, "California corporate agribusiness seized upon racist hysteria and pseudo 'national security' issues . . . so that it could unlawfully seize tens of thousands of acres of productive farm land from law-abiding American citizens."

Gloria Morita's family in Sacramento, California, had a large strawberry and raspberry crop ready to harvest. They sold the crop for a pittance, "together with all the farm equipment, the . . . small truck, the rabbits, chickens, and everything left in the house, including the stove, refrigerator, and furniture, such as beds, dining table and chairs. . . . Papa accepted the $350. Our piano was sold to another vulture for $5."

Eager bargain hunters swarmed into Japanese neighborhoods. A San Francisco newspaper article entitled "Jap Town Sells Out" described this scene: "Along Post St. you can buy anything from a pool table to a begonia plant cheap. . . . The Junkmen are picking over the lamps,

With little notice, Japanese Americans gathered their personal belongings and prepared for evacuation.

rugs, the books and toys that are excess baggage for the Japanese in times like these."

The government offered warehouses to store people's property for the duration of the internment. Some farmers were able to find non-Japanese neighbors to run their farms for them while they were away. More often, though, land dealers bought farmland at enormous discounts. Real estate dealers eyed the evacuees' homes and shops, eager to swoop in and take possession.

How did Japanese Americans maintain their dignity in the face of this outrage? Many accepted it as the workings of fate. The often-quoted response, especially from older people, was *"Shikata ga nai"*—"It can't be helped." Yet, implied in that saying was an ethic of persevering—of carrying on with life in spite of difficulties.

Citizens' Perspectives: A Mixture of Fear and Sadness

Newspaper articles made it appear that most Caucasians welcomed the evacuation. These headlines from the *Los Angeles Times* were typical in the weeks before the evacuation order:

CALIFORNIANS SEEK MORE ALIEN CURBS

NEW WEST COAST RAIDS FEARED

[ABRAHAM] LINCOLN WOULD INTERN JAPS

Such articles appealed to people's fear and patriotism, and many Caucasians fell in line with this thinking.

On the other hand, many others were dismayed, especially those who had nothing to gain when their Japanese American neighbors were interned. For example, after the evacuation, a high school teacher in Oregon suddenly found all her Japanese American students gone. She sadly recalled, "They were my best students." Azalia Peet of Gresham, Oregon, was saddened as well. Having once been a missionary in Japan, she genuinely loved and respected her Japanese American neighbors. "These are law-abiding, upright people of our community," she said. "What is it that makes it necessary for them to evacuate?"

The *San Francisco Chronicle* documented the stark reality of absent residents in an article dated May 21, 1942: "For the first time in 81 years, not a single Japanese is walking the streets of San Francisco."

Assembly Centers

Once the Japanese Americans had been rounded up and registered, those charged with moving this great mass of humanity so quickly had a problem: there was nowhere to put all the detainees. Camps had not yet been built. So the Wartime Civilian Control Agency (WCCA), a branch of the U.S. Army, assigned people to temporary holding pens called Civilian Assembly Centers. There they would stay until they could be moved to long-term detention centers, or internment camps.

Of the seventeen hastily prepared assembly centers, eight were in California, and others stood in Arizona, Oregon, and Washington State. Estelle Ishigo, a Caucasian woman married to a Japanese American man, described her reaction when she first arrived at California's Pomona Assembly Center:

> The first sight of the barbed wire enclosure
> with armed soldiers standing guard as
> our bus slowly turned in through the
> gate stunned us with the meaning of this
> ordered evacuation. Here was a camp of
> sheds, enclosed within a high barbed wire
> fence, with guard towers and soldiers with
> machine guns.

Most assembly centers were converted fairgrounds. Others were at facilities such as horse racetracks, livestock exhibition halls, and migrant worker camps. At the racetracks, horse stalls were cleaned out and turned into living quarters. Nevertheless, the odor of manure still hung in the air. California's Santa Anita racetrack housed 8,500 of its more than 18,000 residents in barns. More than 3,800

Letters to the Editor

According to journalism historian Brian Thornton, most newspapers supported the internment. But what about the readers—the ordinary citizens for whom the papers were published? "The historical record," Thornton says, "is generally bereft of any detailed studies of how newspaper readers responded in 1942 to the Japanese American imprisonment."

Thornton did a study of readers' letters to newspaper editors published in seven West Coast papers plus *The New York Times* from March to June 1942. He found that 70 percent of the letters favored internment. A typical letter from Auburn, Washington, said, "The Japs in Tokyo, no doubt, intended to use the Japs already here as a screen to filter into our midst, then stab us in the back."

A Seattle reader said she enjoyed being "able to pass about the marketplaces without having to hear the monkey-like jabber of a lot of Japs."

Letters opposed to the internment (30 percent) stressed both Americans' rights and their racial prejudice. According to a reader in Alameda, California, Americans should "wake up to gross violations of the Bill of Rights as the Japanese are being hauled away." A California resident wrote to *The New York Times*, "Not since the Civil War have we had such a blow at our whole American ideal as the order to evacuate all Japanese. I think that it is a colossal blunder."

Thornton acknowledges that newspapers pick and choose which letters to publish. Still, the letters reveal the elements and tone of public discussion on the internment.

The Santa Anita race track in Arcadia, California, was converted to an assembly center with barracks built to house more than 18,000 people.

internees lived under one roof at the municipal exhibition hall in Portland, Oregon. The vast arena was divided into separate family spaces.

In most centers, though, people lived in barracks—plain, wooden buildings like those that housed soldiers on military bases. Inside the 100-foot-long barracks, walls divided the space into several partitions, with one large room for each family. By June 1942 more than 110,000 Japanese Americans had been moved into assembly centers.

Relocation Centers

Meanwhile, the War Department was erecting ten permanent relocation centers as fast as workers could build them. All were in isolated areas a "safe" distance from the West Coast. Land quality ranged from arid desert to swampy marshland. Some camps were on privately owned land, while others were taken over from American Indian reservations or other government lands. There were two centers in California and two in Arizona. Colorado, Wyoming, Idaho, and Utah each had a camp, and two were built as far east as Arkansas. The camps were far from large population centers. Often a relocation center was the largest "town" in its area. Camp populations ranged from 7,318 people at Colorado's Amache center to 18,789 at California's Manzanar camp.

Gradually, the internees were transferred by truck, bus, or railroad from assembly centers to their long-term quarters in the internment camps. By November 1942 all the internees had been moved. Young and old, they were destined to spend the next three years of their lives there.

Living conditions in the camps were much the same as they had been in the assembly centers. Row upon row of long wooden barracks stretched out for acres in desolate, barren landscapes. The barracks were grouped into blocks of twelve buildings. Each block had its central mess hall for dining, a recreation building, and a building for toilets, showers, and laundry. Other camp structures were hospitals, post offices, warehouses, administration offices, and schools. Surrounding each camp were barbed wire fences, with armed guards posted in watchtowers. To manage the day-to-day operations of the internment centers, President Roosevelt created the War Relocation Authority (WRA).

A Japanese American family gathers for a meal in the mess hall at the Manzanar, California, relocation center.

It was a civilian agency, with civilian employees, under the supervision of the Department of the Interior.

Daily Life in the Camps

Life behind barbed wire, surrounded by armed guards, was a dehumanizing experience for the internees. Wind, dust, and sand blew in between the cracks of the hastily built barracks, and insects and snakes crept in. Many internees had to adjust to a different climate. For example, the Heart Mountain camp was in Wyoming, where winters are bitterly cold. Internees from California had never experienced such weather, so they were poorly prepared.

The tarpaper-covered barracks buildings had no cooking facilities and no plumbing. They were partitioned so that a whole family occupied a single room measuring about 20 by 25 feet. A lone, bare lightbulb hung from the ceiling in each partition. Beds were cots with straw-stuffed mattresses.

In each block of barracks, as many as 250 people might share the community toilet and shower facilities, which had no partitions. People ate cafeteria-style meals in their block's mess hall. Although each camp had a hospital, there were rarely enough medical supplies, and not enough work-ers were available to take care of several thousand people's needs. Nevertheless, internees worked hard to make their everyday lives as normal as possible. They re-created their communities as well as they could, building the camps into well-functioning little towns.

Residents dressed up their desolate landscapes by plant-ing trees, hedges, and flower gardens around their homes. They received the plants through the WRA or collected them from the surrounding countryside. At most camps, residents produced much of their own food. They operated vegetable farms, and some also raised chickens, pigs, and cows, all from stock provided by the WRA. Many internees were assigned to jobs that helped keep the camps running. There were teachers, cooks, and maintenance, construction, and medical workers. The government paid them from eight to

Special Internment Camps

Japanese Americans were not the only people held in U.S. internment camps during World War II. More than 11,000 people of German ancestry were evacuated as well. Other internees were from Italy, Hungary, Bulgaria, Romania, Czechoslovakia, and Poland. All were considered enemy aliens because their homelands were nations with which the United States was at war.

In addition, the U.S. government asked several Latin American countries to hand over their German residents for security purposes. The governments of these countries complied, and more than four thousand Germans from Latin America were interned. Some were Jewish people who had fled Hitler's regime, which was intent on exterminating Jews.

All these out-of-the-ordinary internees were held at more than fifty special detention camps around the country. The largest camp, located in Crystal City, Texas, did not close until 1947; the last of these special internees was released in 1948.

Internees created communities that mirrored their lives before internment.

nineteen dollars per month, depending on their level of skill. Each camp had a resident governing council that regulated various aspects of community life.

School, Recreation, and Arts

Some camps had ready-made wooden school buildings. In others, the internees built schools for their children with their bare hands. Lumber was in short supply, so they sometimes used mud and straw to make adobe bricks. Each camp was like a school district all its own. Both Caucasian and interned Japanese teachers taught students from grades one through twelve. Books and school supplies were often scarce, and many were donated by charitable organizations.

Residents formed their own sports teams. Baseball was the favorite outdoor sport, and most camps had baseball teams for both females and males. Camp residents also formed civic organizations, card-playing and checkers clubs, and parent-teacher associations. They held dances, showed movies, and organized theater performances. There were

Japanese American students attend school at a relocation center in Idaho.

Female internees enjoy a game of baseball at the Manzanar Relocation Center.

even Boy Scout troops. All these activities helped make life bearable behind barbed wire.

Residents who were gardeners did their best to beautify their new communities. Gathering rocks from the desert, they built rock gardens with mosses, cactus mounds, and stepping-stones. Others used driftwood they had collected to carve benches, tables, and lamps for their family cubicles.

Getting Out

There were a few ways that residents could get permission to leave the camps. For example, some were granted leave to go into the nearest town for shopping. Some cultivated gardens outside the barbed wire and were allowed to go there to farm. Others were given longer leaves for special purposes. With so many of the country's able-bodied men either involved in the war effort or detained in the camps, many Caucasian farmers experienced a shortage of farm labor. Thousands of internees, therefore, were temporarily released to do seasonal agricultural work. Others were selected to work in factories producing war equipment. In some camps, women were released to work as maids for local residents. While some camps were strict about granting leave, others were lax.

Going to college was another way out. This was made possible by the American Friends Service Committee (AFSC), an arm of the Religious Society of Friends, also known as the Quakers. The AFSC, like its parent faith, is opposed to war and committed to human rights. The group found colleges and universities in the Midwestern and eastern United States that were willing to accept Japanese American students. About four thousand college-aged men and women were able to leave the camps under this program.

The Baptist Home Mission Society helped people get out, too. It found families who agreed to sponsor Japanese American families or individuals. The sponsors helped internees find jobs or colleges that would accept them. They also provided a home until the transplanted family could get back on its feet.

Relations with Local Residents

Although the internees were imprisoned, area residents were sometimes resentful of them. After all, from the locals' point

Military Service

Internees who were believed to be loyal were eligible to join the U.S. armed forces. Depending on government regulations at various times, some volunteered and others were drafted. They went into any of three all-Japanese military units. One was the 100th Battalion, whose members originated in Hawaii. Another group formed the Military Intelligence Service (MIS). Their job was to translate Japanese military communications. Some were also involved in interrogating Japanese prisoners.

The third unit was the 442nd Regimental Combat Team, whose members received many medals for their service in combat in Europe. The 442nd eventually became the most decorated unit of its size and length of combat service in U.S. military history.

Paul Tsuneishi voiced the attitude of many draftees: "I knew that there was a Constitutional issue, I knew that there were resisters, but like most Nisei my age I wanted to serve."

of view, the internees were getting more than most people had—free housing and food, as well as running water and electricity. In Colorado's Amache camp, the WRA built a high school for the roughly six hundred high-school-age children who lived there. Residents of nearby Lamar resented the internees because the camp got a new school. Local stores wanted the internees' business, but residents were still wary of the strangers in their midst. To some, the fact that many internees spoke Japanese instead of English made them seem untrustworthy. A Lamar policeman said, "We don't have no trouble with Japs. They're good guys individually. . . . But they're Japanese."

Residents around Wyoming's Heart Mountain camp were even less welcoming. In two nearby towns, the town councils passed a joint resolution affirming that "the visiting of the Japanese in the Towns of Powell and Cody be held to an absolute minimum."

Resentment among locals was not universal, though. Rosalie Gould's family lived near the Rohwer camp in Arkansas during the internment. "I didn't know anything about [the internees]," she said. "Nobody did. People didn't know why they were there, if they were prisoners of war or what." Still, relations between the locals and the internees were exceptionally friendly. For example, internees taught local farmers how to irrigate their fields and introduced them to new crops, such as eggplant.

Relations among children were good, too. "The young people would go out and camp on the Arkansas River with the Boy Scouts. They played football and basketball with the Caucasian children and would go swimming," Gould remembers. "As long as they could play," she says of the interned children, "they were content."

Four

Voices of Dissent

THE MAJORITY OF THE INTERNEES accepted their confinement without protest. Former internee Janet Baba believes that cultural traditions and attitudes such as respect for authority were mainly responsible for this passivity. Those who did protest chose various avenues. Some voiced their dissent through riots, demonstrations, and strikes. Others chose civil disobedience, or nonviolent refusal to obey laws they believed were unjust. They defied curfews, evacuation orders, and the military draft. Some of them fought their battles in the nation's courts.

Protests, Riots, and Strikes

Among camp residents, there were different factions with different feelings about their internment. Most residents quietly went along with the internment process. Nisei who belonged to the JACL were especially cooperative with their government overseers.

On the other hand, some of the older Issei, who as immigrants had been denied U.S. citizenship, were resentful. Although the vast majority condemned the Pearl Harbor attack, the Issei retained strong cultural ties with Japan, and they still loved their homeland. A third group, the *Kibei,* were young Japanese Americans who had been born in the United States, like the Nisei, but educated in Japan. Their feelings occupied a sort of middle ground.

The various factions distrusted one another and sometimes clashed. Men were known to roam the camps at night and beat suspected informants with clubs and canes. Caucasian camp officials became targets of suspicion, too, as possible informants. These tensions added to the discontent over living conditions and rules. They sometimes led to protests, strikes, and outright riots.

Wyoming's Heart Mountain camp was the center of a draft resistance movement. In 1944, when internees began to be drafted for military service, a group of men formed the Heart Mountain Fair Play Committee and refused to be drafted. Frank Emi, who led the resisters, voiced their perspective: "I could not believe that the government could actually put us in camp, strip us of everything . . . and then order us into the military as if nothing had happened."

An editorial in the *Heart Mountain Sentinel*, the JACL-run camp newspaper, called the resisters "deluded youth" and blamed the Issei for influencing them: "We frankly believe some of our parents are skating on thin ice in their relations with their adopted country." Seven draft resistance leaders were later convicted of conspiracy, and more than eighty internees were imprisoned for evading the draft.

The Topaz camp in Utah had its troubles, too. In April 1943 a guard saw sixty-three-year-old James Wasaka standing near the fence. Thinking Wasaka was trying to escape, the guard shot the internee and killed him. Residents organized a strike until after Wasaka's funeral.

Tule Lake, the high-security facility, was a hotbed of discontent. In November 1943 an estimated 5,000 to 10,000

The Loyalty Questionnaire

A major source of discontent in the camps was the loyalty questionnaire. All internees over the age of seventeen were required to fill it out. The most controversial questions were 27 and 28:

27. Are you willing to serve in the armed forces of the United States on combat duty, wherever ordered? (Women were asked if they would join the Women's Army Corps [WACs] or the Army Nurses Corps.)

28. Will you swear unqualified allegiance to the United States of America and faithfully defend the United States from any or all attack by foreign or domestic forces, and foreswear any form of allegiance or obedience to the Japanese emperor, or any other foreign government, power, or organization?

Those who failed were deemed to be disloyal. They were held in California's Tule Lake camp, a high-security segregation center for those considered to be dangerous enemies.

internees swarmed around the administration offices. They were protesting poor sanitation, unsafe working conditions, and lack of proper medical care. Martial law was imposed, with the U.S. Army bringing in machine guns and tanks until things settled down in January.

The most serious upheaval was an incident that occurred on December 5–6, 1942, called the Manzanar Riot. Rumors had been circulating through Manzanar that camp officials were stealing meat and sugar and selling these valuable commodities outside the camp. Anger over these rumors laid the groundwork for the riot. When a Japanese American kitchen worker was arrested for allegedly beating up a JACL member, thousands of internees marched on the administration building in protest. Military police threw tear gas and fired into the crowd, killing a seventeen-year-old boy. Another man who had been wounded died later.

Supreme Court Challenges

Meanwhile, other forms of protest were working their way through the legal system in the nation's courtrooms. Most were based on the principles outlined in the U.S. Constitution, particularly the first ten amendments, or Bill of Rights. Throughout the 1940s the JACL and the ACLU tried to challenge the internment in court. Several Japanese Americans who had been arrested for violating internment laws agreed to let their situations become test cases. The next step was to file lawsuits against the government, citing violations of the Constitution. Four of those cases reached the U.S. Supreme Court.

The case of *Hirabayashi v. United States* involved Gordon Hirabayashi of Seattle, a student at the University of Washington. When a curfew of 8:00 PM was imposed on Japanese

Americans, he deliberately stayed out later. He also refused to register for evacuation to an internment camp. He was then arrested, convicted, and jailed for these offenses.

Hirabayashi felt that if he had obeyed the camp rules, he would have given up his rights as an American citizen. In appealing his case, he argued that it was unconstitutional for Congress to let the army impose regulations such as curfews and exclusion orders. He also claimed that the government had violated his Fifth Amendment right to due process, or normal legal procedures. Hirabayashi also argued that, in singling out one ethnic group, the government had violated the guarantee of equal protection under the law provided by the Fourteenth Amendment.

The Supreme Court ruled against Hirabayashi. It said that the Constitution gave the president and Congress the power to wage war as they saw fit. It affirmed that special measures were needed during wartime and that the military had good reason to be suspicious of Japanese Americans. Therefore, the curfew and evacuation orders were not based on race alone. However, the court did not address the issue of whether the internment itself was or was not constitutional.

The case of *Yasui v. United States* was similar, with some unique features. Like Hirabayashi, Minoru Yasui of Portland deliberately violated both the curfew and the evacuation order. His perspective was somewhat different, though, as he was a lawyer. Also, he had once worked for the Japanese consulate in Chicago. When General DeWitt issued the curfew order in March 1942, Yasui was shocked. "The thing that struck me immediately," he recalled, "was that the military was ordering the civilian to do something. In my opinion, that's the way dictatorships are formed." As he expected, Yasui was arrested and imprisoned. Being a lawyer, he was eager to use his case to test the constitutionality of these measures.

A lower court ruled that the curfew was indeed unconstitutional if applied to American citizens. However, the court also said that Yasui had renounced his American citizenship by actions such as working for the Japanese consulate. Therefore, Yasui was reclassified as an enemy alien. For failing to comply with applicable orders, he was fined and sent to jail. When the case reached the Supreme Court, the justices overturned much of what the lower court had decided. However, they upheld Yasui's original conviction for violating the curfew.

In *Korematsu v. United States*, the Supreme Court again avoided the issue of the internment's constitutionality, as it had in *Hirabayashi*. Fred Korematsu of Oakland, California, became a fugitive when evacuation orders were issued. He had plastic surgery to alter his appearance, changed his name, and went into hiding. Authorities found him, arrested him, and put him in jail.

In court, Korematsu argued that no one should be imprisoned, or interned, without having a trial to determine the accused person's loyalty or disloyalty. He based this on the Fifth Amendment's guarantee of due process. Like Hirabayashi, Korematsu also raised the issue of racial discrimination.

Supreme Court justice Hugo Black said that the charge of racial prejudice "merely confuses the issue." The war, the uncertain loyalties of Japanese Americans, and military necessity justified the exclusion order. Justice Frank Murphy, in one of four separate dissenting opinions, strongly disagreed:

This exclusion of "all persons of Japanese ancestry, both alien and non-alien," from the Pacific Coast area on a plea of military necessity in the absence of martial law ought not to be approved. Such exclusion goes over "the very brink of constitutional power" and falls into the ugly abyss of racism.

Nevertheless, in a 6–3 decision handed down on December 18, 1944, the Supreme Court upheld Korematsu's conviction for having violated the evacuation order.

Fred Korematsu (left), Minoru Yasui (center), and Gordon Hirabayashi (right), were each involved in landmark U.S. Supreme Court cases that challenged the internment of Japanese Americans during World War II.

Internees finally scored a Supreme Court victory in the case entitled *Ex parte Endo.* It involved Mitsuye Endo, who had been a secretary in Sacramento, California. She was sent to the Tule Lake internment camp. From there, she had her lawyer file a legal motion called a writ of habeas corpus, which was an important step in determining whether her imprisonment was lawful. Endo was demanding to be either charged with a crime or released.

Government officials agreed that Endo was a loyal citizen and that there were no specific charges against her. The U.S. government, hoping to make a deal, offered to release Endo in some other location, away from the West Coast. She refused. She felt it was her right to return to her own home. Endo spent two more years in internment before the case reached the Supreme Court.

This time, the Court's opinion was unanimous. It ruled that the detention of citizens known to be loyal was unconstitutional. The Court also dealt a blow to the racial aspect of the internment: "Loyalty is a matter of the heart and mind not of race, creed, or color. . . . Mitsuye Endo is entitled to an unconditional release by the War Relocation Authority."

This ruling, issued on December 18, 1944, the same day as the *Korematsu* decision, was a major step toward closing the camps and ending the internment nightmare for Japanese Americans.

Five

Release, Redress, and Reparations

As WORLD WAR II WORE ON, the Allies continued to fight on two fronts—in Europe and in the Pacific. By late 1944 the Allies had scored one victory after another in Pacific battles. It seemed certain that Japan's power was waning. On December 17, 1944, the U.S. Army issued Public Proclamation No. 21. It announced that Japanese Americans were no longer a threat to military security. They were free to go home. That was just one day before the Supreme Court ruling that the government could not detain loyal citizens without charging them. The release was set to begin on January 2, 1945. By October or November 1945 most camps were deserted. Tule Lake was the last to close, with the last residents leaving in March 1946.

A New Beginning

Upon release, internees prepared for a new beginning. They were given an allowance of twenty-five dollars each and one-way train fare to their destination. Some settled in cities scattered across the country. If a family member had settled in the Midwestern or eastern United States, the rest of the family joined him or her. Some emigrated to Japan when they were released. Most of the internees, however, went back to the cities and towns they had left three years earlier.

The End of the War

As the camps were closing, World War II was winding down as well. The war in Europe ended on May 8, 1945, when Germany formally surrendered to the Allies. This date is remembered as V-E Day.

President Roosevelt, who had presided over both the war and the internment, did not live to see this victory. He died on April 12, 1945, at the age of sixty-three. Roosevelt's vice president, Harry Truman, was quickly sworn in as president.

On August 6 and 9, 1945, Truman directed the U.S. Army Air Forces to drop the world's first atomic bombs on the Japanese cities of Hiroshima and Nagasaki. The effects were devastating. Emperor Hirohito of Japan announced his surrender on August 15, with the formal surrender taking place on September 2—V-J Day. World War II was over at last.

Few, however, were able to take up their old lives again. Much of what they had left behind had been lost, stolen, or destroyed. Even property left for safekeeping in government storage was largely gone. Only about one-fourth of those who had owned farms before the internment still had their property. Even then, their farms were overgrown with weeds, their farm machinery rusty or gone. Paul Shinoda remembers: "We couldn't pack up all the stoves and refrigerators and stuff like that. We stored them away in the nursery—our stove, our kids' toys, and some of our furniture. Some truck driver took our stove and never paid for it. When we got back from camp we had nothing—even the toys were all gone."

A Japanese American family returns to their home in Seattle, Washington, after internment to find it vandalized with anti-Japanese graffiti.

Rediscovering History

Throughout the 1950s the former internees got on with rebuilding their lives. Adults grew older, and children grew up and started careers and families of their own. Hoping to close a sordid chapter of their history, older Japanese Americans tended not to talk about their internment. The youngest internees, who had left the camps as infants, had little or no memory of the episode.

Between the very young and the very old were many who remembered the camps but preferred to focus on their new lives instead. They were pleased to see their own children embracing school, sports, entertainment, and other features of American culture they had not been able to enjoy.

Little by little, young Japanese Americans began to learn about their families' hidden histories. For former internees and their children alike, the civil rights movement of the 1960s was inspiring. African Americans were focusing on their ethnic identity, their history, and their rights as American citizens. This motivated young Japanese Americans to embark on the same quest. In 1963 members of the JACL joined Dr. Martin Luther King Jr. on his march to Washington, D.C. This was a way to show their commitment to full civil rights for all Americans.

The Road to Redress

Gradually, the Japanese American community focused more public attention on the internment. In 1976 President Gerald Ford officially rescinded Executive Order 9066, which had initiated the internment. In a public White House ceremony he called the episode a national mistake.

In 1978 the JACL launched a campaign for redress—
that is, for righting the wrongs that the internment had done.
Members called for a formal apology from the government
and $25,000 per internee. They also called for an education
fund to teach the public about the internment in hopes that
such a thing would never happen again.

In 1980, under President Jimmy Carter, Congress
created the Commission on Wartime Relocation and Internment of Civilians. Its job was to investigate the internment.
The commission issued its report, entitled *Personal Justice
Denied*, in 1983. It concluded that "the causes of the internment were race prejudice, wartime hysteria and a failure of
political leadership." The committee recommended that the

President Jimmy Carter signs an act creating the Commission on Wartime
Relocation and Internment of Civilians on July 30, 1980.

Personal Justice Denied
(excerpt)

Executive Order 9066 was not justified by military necessity, and the decisions which followed from it—detention, ending detention and ending exclusion—were not driven by analysis of military conditions. The broad historical causes which shaped these decisions were race prejudice, war hysteria and a failure of political leadership. Widespread ignorance of Japanese Americans contributed to [the tragic results of] a policy conceived in haste and executed in an atmosphere of fear and anger at Japan. A grave injustice was done to American citizens and resident aliens of Japanese ancestry who, without individual review or any probative evidence against them, were excluded, removed and detained by the United States during World War II.

government issue an apology for the internment, pay $20,000 to each of the roughly 60,000 surviving internees, and create an education fund.

Opposing Views

As in the past, not everyone in the Japanese American community was inclined to condemn the internment. Attorney Ken Masugi, whose parents had been interned, testified before Congress in opposition to the relocation commission's recommendations:

> The major problem [with the report]
> is that of the arrogance of hindsight.
> The Commission tended to label as 'war
> hysteria' what reasonable men saw at the
> time as natural responses to dramatic,
> disturbing events. . . . Ethnic heritage has
> traditionally affected the foreign policy
> views of Americans. . . . [T]he ethnic
> Japanese are no different from other ethnic
> groups in this regard . . . .

A small minority in the Japanese American community agreed with former California senator S. I. Hayakawa, who believed that the internment was reasonable under the circumstances. In his testimony he said:

> Of course the relocation was unjust. But
> under the stress of wartime anxieties and in
> the light of the long history of anti-Oriental

agitation in California and the West, I find it difficult to imagine what else could have occurred that would not have been many times worse.

Correcting Legal Errors

At the time, there were four Japanese American members of Congress — senators Daniel Inouye and Spark Matsunaga of Hawaii and representatives Norman Mineta and Robert Matsui of California. They took the lead in persuading others in Congress to approve the committee's recommendations. However, approval did not come right away. Some members of Congress felt it was wrong to condemn the mistakes of an earlier generation of Americans. Others objected because the Supreme Court had ruled in the 1940s that the internment was legal.

Teams of lawyers, meanwhile, were busy trying to get federal courts to reverse those very Supreme Court decisions. In each case, they filed a petition for a *writ of error coram nobis*, a rarely used legal action asserting that errors had been made. All three cases were reversed. A federal district court in San Francisco overturned Fred Korematsu's conviction in 1984. A Portland, Oregon, court vacated Minoru Yasui's conviction in 1986. By 1987 courts in Seattle had overturned Gordon Hirabayashi's convictions.

Several legal errors were cited in these postwar rulings. Government attorneys in the original cases had withheld evidence or lied to the court. They had concealed General DeWitt's blatantly racial diatribes about people of Japanese ancestry. They had also suppressed DeWitt's reports that no Japanese

Americans had ever committed espionage or sabotage. There had been no military necessity for the internment at all.

Finally, after five years of delays, Congress approved the relocation committee's recommendations by passing the Civil Liberties Act of 1988. President Ronald Reagan signed the act into law on August 10, 1988, and reparation payments began in 1990.

Congressmen surround President Ronald Reagan as he signs the Civil Liberties Act into law in 1988.

Protesting an Apology

For twelve years after the Civil Liberties Act, members of the Japanese American Citizens League debated whether they should issue an apology of their own. Many members felt the JACL had been wrong in suppressing the voices of internees who had resisted the military draft during World War II and for snubbing them and their families. Finally, at the JACL's national convention in Monterey, California, in the year 2000, members voted 2–1 to issue this apology.

After the measure was passed, several older JACL members walked out of the meeting and vowed to cancel their memberships. Tak Tsutsui expressed the protesters' viewpoint: "In my mind, they're draft dodgers. To me, you don't honor draft dodgers. . . . you recognize those who went to fight for this country and for the Japanese who were in those camps." This is typical of internment controversies that still divide the Japanese American community.

Memorials

Many memorials now honor Japanese Americans for their experiences during World War II. One of these memorials stirred up passionate controversy within the Japanese American community. In 2000 the National Park Service (NPS) erected a Japanese American Memorial to Patriotism During World War II in Washington, D.C. Its inscription praised the Nisei who had served in the war, lauded former JACL leader Mike Masaoka for his patriotism, and included a quote from Masaoka's Japanese American Creed. Protests arose in the Japanese American community, as many felt Masaoka had betrayed their interests by supporting the internment. The NPS made minor changes, but it kept the reference to Masaoka and the creed, so the protests continue.

Other memorials honor the internees and their hardships in the camps. Most of the former internment camps have been designated as historic places within the National Park System. In 1992 the Manzanar camp was declared a National Historic Site, and the Rohwer camp became a National Historic Landmark. The Minidoka camp was designated a National Historic Site in 2001. In 2006 the Tule Lake, Granada, and Heart Mountain camps became National Historic Landmarks, and the Topaz camp received the same designation in 2007.

In 1998 in a White House ceremony, President Bill Clinton awarded Fred Korematsu the Presidential Medal of Freedom—the highest honor that the country gives to a U.S. civilian. In his remarks, Clinton said, "[Korematsu] had his conviction overturned in federal court, empowering tens of thousands of Japanese Americans and giving him

Offerings hang on the barbed-wire fence surrounding the cemetery at Manzanar, a National Historic Site since 1992.

what he said he wanted most of all, the chance to feel like an American once again."

The citation inscribed on the award was equally inspiring: "Fred Korematsu challenged our Nation's conscience, reminding us that we must uphold the rights of our own citizens even as we fight tyranny in other lands."

Six

Never Again?

Those who cannot remember the past are condemned to repeat it.
— Novelist and philosopher George Santayana

EVEN TODAY THE INTERNMENT ISSUE remains both relevant and controversial. Are unconstitutional acts by the government ever justified? Should we ignore the Constitution during war or other national emergencies? How much power should a president have during wartime? Enough power to throw out the Constitution?

Silent Laws, Inhuman Mistakes

A Latin proverb says, *Inter arma silent leges* — "In time of war the laws are silent." One recent chief justice of the United States, William Rehnquist, believed there was some truth to that saying. He pointed out that judges rarely rule against wartime measures while the war is going on. Instead, they tend to take a stand for civil liberties only *after* a war is over. That is clearly what happened in the case of the Japanese American internment. During the war, judges upheld the constitutionality of the internment; after the war, they overruled it.

There is a price to pay for treating the Constitution so casually. It is shame, regret, and the bitter, nagging judgment of hindsight. Supreme Court justice William O. Douglas had voted against Fred Korematsu in his 1944 appeal. In his autobiography, Douglas said he had always regretted his decision. "Grave injustices had been committed. Fine American citizens had been robbed of their properties by racists. . . . The evacuation case . . . was ever on my conscience."

California attorney general Earl Warren had been one of the leading voices in urging the evacuation. Later he led the Supreme Court as chief justice. Warren expressed regret in his autobiography, as well:

> I have since deeply regretted the removal
> order and my own testimony advocating
> it, because it was not in keeping with our

After re-evaluating their decisions, Supreme Court Justices William Douglas (left) and Earl Warren (right), admitted that grave injustices were committed against Japanese Americans during World War II.

American concept of freedom and the
rights of citizens. Whenever I thought of
the innocent little children who were torn
from home, school friends and congenial
surroundings, I was conscience-stricken.

Milton Eisenhower, the first director of the War Relocation Authority, could not stand what he was doing. Acting
without the benefit of hindsight, he quit after only four
months, telling his successor, "I can't sleep and do this job. I
had to get out of it." Eisenhower later called the evacuation
"an inhuman mistake."

A New Target Group

It is easy to pass off the internment as an unfortunate but
uncharacteristic episode in American history. The mass
imprisonment of one ethnic group probably will never happen here again. However, whenever the country is gripped
with fear, constitutional rights are in danger of falling by the
wayside.

This issue came up again after September 11, 2001, when
terrorists hijacked airplanes and crashed them into buildings
in New York City and Washington, D.C. The climate of fear
and prejudice that followed is often compared to the conditions that led to the internment.

Because the terrorists were Muslim Arabs, the events of
September 11 unleashed fear and suspicion against American
Muslims and people of Middle Eastern or South Asian ori-
gin. Individuals beat and even killed people they suspected
of belonging to these groups. Hate blogs flourished on the
Internet. Airport security guards practiced racial profiling,

After the September 11, 2001, terrorist attacks, many American Muslims experienced racial profiling. Here Moslem men pray at Tampa International Airport in Florida.

considering people dangerous because of their ethnic appearance. Again, civil liberties and constitutional rights took a backseat to suspicion.

As in the 1940s, the government took drastic actions in the name of national security. In 2001 Congress passed the USA Patriot Act, also known as the Anti-Terrorism Bill. It gave government agencies broad power to access phone and e-mail communications, detain both citizens and noncitizens indefinitely without charges, and even find out from bookstores and libraries what people were reading. Many parts of the act were revised or eliminated in 2005 and 2006. Nevertheless, Americans have long been gravely divided over its sweeping provisions. In a December 2004 opinion poll conducted by Cornell University, 44 percent of all respondents believed the government should restrict the civil liberties of Muslim Americans in some way.

Anti-Terrorism Meets the Internment

As with the internment, several lawsuits challenging the Patriot Act were brought before the Supreme Court. The plaintiffs asserted that they were being imprisoned unlawfully as enemy combatants. Fred Korematsu joined in filing statements with the court, warning that history was repeating itself:

> by allowing the Executive Branch to decide
> unilaterally who to detain, and for how long,
> our country will repeat the same mistakes of
> the past.

> The extreme nature of the government's
> position is all-too-familiar. . . . [H]istory
> teaches that we tend too quickly to sacrifice
> these liberties in the face of overbroad claims
> of military necessity.

In almost all the cases challenging the Patriot Act, the Supreme Court has ruled that the plaintiffs should not be held without charges.

The Patriot Act: Opposing Views

Senator Russ Feingold of Wisconsin voiced his opposition to the act from the Senate floor:

Preserving our freedom is one of the main reasons that we are now engaged in this new war on terrorism. We will lose that war without firing a shot if we sacrifice the liberties of the American people. . . . I believe [the bill] falls short of meeting even basic constitutional standards of due process and fairness. The bill continues to allow the Attorney General to detain persons based on mere suspicion. . . . The bill also continues to deny detained persons a trial or hearing. . . .

On the other hand, attorneys John Yoo and Eric Posner supported the act as a necessary safeguard:

> *[The act] creates no revolution in government powers, nor does it violate the Constitution. If the act marginally reduces peacetime liberties, this is a reasonable price to pay for a valuable weapon against al Qaeda, a resourceful and adaptable enemy that is skilled at escaping detection. . . . [The act's provisions] are modest and are worth the small, perhaps even imaginary, reduction in civil liberties. . . . Civil liberties throughout our history have always expanded in peacetime and contracted during emergencies.*

Lessons to Ponder

What have we learned from the Japanese American internment? At least we have seen that fear and prejudice can lead to mass movements against an entire group of people.

Everyone belongs to some group. People could be classified according to culture, religion, ethnicity, gender, age, physical characteristics, clothing, opinions, or even the kinds of recreation and entertainment they like.

Using these criteria, think of all the groups you yourself belong to. Suppose some event or circumstance triggers discomfort or anxiety about one of those groups. Next come fear, suspicion, prejudice, hatred, and active hostility. Imagine those attitudes sweeping the nation, even reaching up to

The Japanese American internment denied many U.S. citizens their constitutional rights, placing them behind barbed wire on the basis of fear and hatred

the government level. Before long, constitutional rights to personal freedom, security in your own home, the protection of U.S. laws, and proper legal procedures are gone. Is this a preposterous scenario, or a believable one?

Living in the United States, we tend to take our constitutional rights for granted. Without our realizing it, they are part of our outlook. Yet, these rights sometimes hang by a thread. When fear and hatred are involved, powerful forces of public opinion can snap that thread.

A monument stands at the Poston Relocation Center in Arizona. It honors the Japanese Americans who were interned at Poston and those who died in World War II. The words inscribed there are both cautionary and inspiring:

> May [this memorial] serve as a constant
> reminder of our past so that Americans
> in the future will never again be denied
> their constitutional rights and may the
> remembrance of that experience serve to
> advance the evolution of the human spirit.

Timeline

1907   Gentlemen's Agreement stops immigration of Japanese workers.

1922   The U.S. Supreme Court confirms that Japanese immigrants cannot become U.S. citizens.

1924   The Immigration Act of 1924 suspends Japanese immigration.

1940   The Alien Registration Act of 1940 requires noncitizens to register with the government.

1941   DECEMBER 7: Japanese bombers attack the U.S. naval base at Pearl Harbor, Hawaii

DECEMBER 8: The United States declares war on Japan, entering World War II.

1942   FEBRUARY 19: President Franklin D. Roosevelt issues Executive Order 9066 providing for exclusion zones, which leads to the evacuation of Japanese Americans from the West Coast.

MARCH 2: Public Proclamation No. 1 announces the locations of the first exclusion zones.

MARCH 21: Congress passes Public Law 503, making it a crime to disobey Executive Order 9066.

MARCH 24: Civilian Exclusion Order No. 1 begins the evacuations.

JUNE: All internees have been moved to temporary Civilian Assembly Centers.

NOVEMBER: All internees have been transferred to ten relocation centers.

DECEMBER: The Manzanar Riot breaks out in California's Manzanar camp.

1943 FEBRUARY: The War Relocation Authority requires internees to fill out a loyalty questionnaire.

APRIL: A guard shoots and kills James Wakasa in Utah's Topaz camp; internees go on strike.

JUNE 21: In *Hirabayashi v. United States* and *Yasui v. United States*, the U.S. Supreme Court rules that curfews for a minority group during wartime are constitutional.

NOVEMBER: More than five thousand internees stage a protest at California's Tule Lake camp.

1944 At Wyoming's Heart Mountain camp, the Fair Play Committee leads a military draft resistance movement; more than eighty resisters are convicted and imprisoned

DECEMBER 18: In *Korematsu v. United States*, the Supreme Court rules that Executive Order 9066 is constitutional; in *Ex parte Endo*, the court rules that loyal U.S. citizens cannot be detained.

1945 JANUARY 2: Release of internees from relocation camps begins.

1946 MARCH: With the closing of the Tule Lake camp, all internees have been released.

1976 President Gerald Ford repeals Executive Order 9066, calling the internment a national mistake.

1978 The Japanese American Citizens League (JACL) launches a campaign for redress.

1980 Congress creates the Commission on Wartime Relocation and Internment of Civilians (CWRIC) to investigate the internment.

1983 CWRIC's report, *Personal Justice Denied*, finds the internment unjustified and recommends reparations.

1984–1988 Federal courts formally vacate the Supreme Court's *Hirabayashi, Yasui,* and *Korematsu* decisions.

1988 The Civil Liberties Act of 1988 grants reparations to surviving Japanese American internees.

1992 The Manzanar camp in California is declared a National Historic Site; the Rohwer camp in Arkansas becomes a National Historic Landmark.

1998 President Bill Clinton awards Fred Korematsu the Presidential Medal of Freedom.

2000 President Clinton awards members of the 442nd Regiment the Congressional Medal of Honor.

2001 The Minidoka camp in Idaho is declared a National Historic Site.

2006 Tule Lake Segregation Center in California, the Granada (Amache) camp in Colorado, and the Heart Mountain camp in Wyoming are declared National Historic Landmarks.

2007 The Topaz camp in Utah becomes a National Historic Landmark.

2008 President George W. Bush announces the World War II Valor in the Pacific National Monument, which will include California's Tule Lake site.

Notes

Chapter One

p. 10, "By 1890 . . .": *The Brown Quarterly*, vol. 3, no. 4 (Spring 2000). The Brown Foundation. http://brownvboard.org/brwnqurt/03-4/03-4a.htm (accessed 4 August 2009).

p. 11, *"The Yellow Peril . . . American Women"*: Roger Daniels, *Asian America: Chinese and Japanese in the United States since 1850* (Seattle, WA: University of Washington Press, 1990), p. 116.

p. 13, "By 1940, 126,947 people . . .": Toshio Yatsushiro, "The Japanese Americans," in *American Minorities: A Textbook of Readings in Intergroup Relations*, ed. Milton L. Barron (New York: Knopf, 1957), p. 319.

p. 13, "Among the 93,717 . . .": "Rumbles from the Coast," *Time*, 23 February 1942, www.time.com/time/magazine/article/0,9171,884436,00.html?promoid=googlep (accessed 5 May 2009).

p. 14, ". . . 157,905 people . . .": Stephan Thernstrom, *Harvard Encyclopedia of American Ethnic Groups* (Cambridge, MA: Harvard University Press, 1980), p. 562.

p. 16, "when war breaks out . . .": *Behind Barbed Wire at Amache*, "History," University of Denver, www.du.edu/behindbarbedwire/history.html (accessed 4 May 2009).

p. 17, "The continued presence . . .": Lt. Gen. J. L. DeWitt to the Chief of Staff, U.S. Army, 5 June 1943, in U.S. Army, Western Defense Command and Fourth Army, *Final Report; Japanese Evacuation from the West Coast 1942* (Washington, D.C.: Govt. Printing Office, 1943), pp. vii–x, www.sfmuseum.net/war/dewitt0.html (accessed 1 May 2009).

p. 18, "First, . . . on the Negro.": Ken Ringle, "What Did You Do before the War, Daddy?" *Washington Post Magazine*, December 6, 1981, p. 56, quoted in Tetsuden Kashima, *Judgment without Trial* (Seattle: University of Washington Press, 2003), pp. 36–37.

p. 18, "[T]here is no Japanese "problem" . . .": Kashima, *Judgment without Trial*, p. 40.

p. 19, "Skull pattern, . . . behavior.": Christopher Thome, *Allies of a Kind: The United States, Britain, and the War Against Japan, 1941–1945* (New York: Oxford University Press, 1978), p. 8, quoted in Geoffrey S. Smith, "Racial Nativism and Origins of Japanese American Relocation," in *Japanese Americans, from Relocation to Redress*, ed. Roger Daniels, Sandra C. Taylor, and Harry H. L. Kitano (Seattle: University of Washington Press, 1991), p. 80.

p. 19, ". . . liable to restraint.": Presidential Proclamation, Aliens, No. 2525, *The Freedom of Information Times*, www.foitimes.com/internment/Proc2525.html (accessed 5 May 2009).

p. 19, "Yesterday . . . Japanese Empire.": "Franklin D. Roosevelt's 'Day of Infamy' Speech," www.ibiblio.org/hyperwar/PTO/EastWind/Infamy.html (accessed 3 May 2009).

Chapter Two

p. 21, "I was walking . . .": Deborah Gesensway and Mindy Roseman, *Beyond Words: Images from America's Concentration Camps* (Ithaca, NY: Cornell University Press, 1987), p. 136.

p. 22, "I turned on the radio . . .": Gesensway and Roseman, *Beyond Words*, p. 135.

p. 22, "we were frightened . . .": "Mary Tsukamoto: Jerome," in *And Justice for All: An Oral History of the Japanese American Detention Camps*, by John Tateishi (Seattle: University of Washington Press, 1999), p. 7.

p. 23, "I am strongly opposed . . . wrong channels.": James Omura, *Japanese American Voice*, www.javoice.com/ (accessed 11 August 2009).

p. 24, Mike Masaoka, "The Japanese American Creed," *Japanese American Voice*, www.javoice.com/masaoka.html (accessed 26 May 2009).

p. 26, "Papers, documents . . .": Presidential Proclamation, Aliens, No. 2525.

p. 26, "When I heard . . .": quoted in Gesensway and Roseman, *Beyond Words*, p. 136.

p. 26, "The attack had . . .": Barry Saiki, "The Uprooting of My Two Communities," in *Japanese Americans, from Relocation to Redress*, ed. Roger Daniels et al., p. 15.

p. 27, "When I got home . . .": Yoshiko Uchida, *Desert Exile: The Uprooting of a Japanese American Family* (Seattle, WA: University of Washington Press, 1984), p. 46.

p. 27, ". . . more than 1,200 Issei . . .": University of Washington Libraries, "Interrupted Lives: Can't Believe It's True — Pearl Harbor," www.lib.washington.edu/exhibits/harmony/UW-new/one/ (accessed 5 May 2009).

p. 28, "In an opinion poll . . . Europe.": Geoffrey S. Smith, "Racial Nativism and Origins of Japanese American

Relocation," in *Japanese Americans, from Relocation to Redress*, ed. Roger Daniels et al., p. 84.

p. 28, "Nobody . . . being there.": Geoffrey S. Smith, "Racial Nativism," p. 82.

p. 28, ". . . producing 10 percent . . .": Executive Order 9066, "Document Info," www.ourdocuments.gov/doc. php?doc=74 (accessed 4 May 2009).

p. 28, "We're charged . . . either.": Frank J. Taylor, "The People Nobody Wants," *Saturday Evening Post*, 9 May 1942, p. 66, quoted in *Toyosaburo Korematsu v. United States*, 323 U.S. 214 (1944), Justice Murphy's dissent, n12, http://laws.findlaw.com/us/323/214.html (accessed 5 May 2009).

p. 29, ". . . [Caucasian] neighbors were watching . . .": "Mary Tsukamoto: Jerome," p. 7.

p. 29, "The necessity for mass evacuation . . .": J. Edgar Hoover, Memo to the Attorney General, 2 February 1942, *The Japanese American Internment*, www.geocities.com/ Athens/8420/politicians.html (accessed 26 May 2009).

p. 30, "A great many West Coast people . . .": Francis Biddle, Memo to Roosevelt, 17 February 1942, *The Japanese American Internment*, www.geocities.com/Athens/8420/ politicians.html (accessed 26 May 2009).

p. 30, "The Japanese race . . .": quoted in *Behind Barbed Wire at Amache*, "Decision to Evacuate" (accessed 4 May 2009).

p. 31, "While it is believed . . .": Lt. Gen. J. L. DeWitt, *Final Report*, Chapters 1 and 2, www.sfmuseum.net/war/ dewitt1.html (accessed 1 May 2009).

p. 32, "We feel that treating . . .": quoted in Marc Dollinger, *Quest for Inclusion* (Princeton, NJ: Princeton University Press, 2000), p. 250.

p. 32, "[T]his is no time . . .": quoted in Ellen Eisenberg, "As Truly American as Your Son: Voicing Opposition to Internment in Three West Coast Cities," *Oregon Historical Quarterly*, 22 December 2003, www.historycooperative. org/journals/ohq/104.4/eisenberg.html (accessed 5 May 2009).

p. 33, "[T]he Japanese population . . .": United States Commission on Wartime Relocation and Internment of Civilians, quoted in *Personal Justice Denied* (Seattle: University of Washington Press, 1997), p. 97.

p. 34, Executive Order 9066 (accessed 4 May 2009).

Chapter Three

p. 35, ". . . the *San Francisco News* reported . . .": "Japanese on West Coast Face Wholesale Uprooting," *San Francisco News*, 4 March 1942, Virtual Museum of the City of San Francisco, www.sfmuseum.net/hist8/intern13.html (accessed 7 May 2009).

p. 37, ". . . at least one-sixteenth . . .": Jeffery F. Burton, Mary M. Farrell, Eleanor Roosevelt, Florence B. Lord, and Irene J. Cohen, *Confinement and Ethnicity: An Overview of World War II Japanese American Relocation Sites* (Seattle: University of Washington Press, 2002), p. 34.

p. 37, ". . . evacuees also included . . . sixty-five years of age,": *Confinement and Ethnicity*, p. 34.

p. 38, "California corporate agribusiness . . .": A. V. Krebs, "Banishment from the 'Gold Mountain'," *Agriculture and Human Values* 12, no. 3 (June 1995), p. 45, www.springerlink.com/index/P087580542P40164.pdf (accessed 5 May 2009).

p. 38, "together with all the farm equipment . . .": "Gloria Morita on the Manzanar Internment," quoted in Institute for Leadership Development and Study of Pacific and Asian North American Religion, www.panainstitute.org/nisei-gloria-morita-manzanar-eo-9066 (accessed 7 May 2009).

p. 38, ". . . Jap Town Sells Out . . .": "WWII The Good War," History 1308, Week 10_04, UMN 3/31/04. www.hist.umn.edu/~sargent/1308/out%20week%2010_04.htm (accessed 7 May 2009).

p. 40, *"Californians Seek . . . Intern Japs"*: S. Mintz, "Explorations: Japanese American Internment," *Digital History,* 2007,www.digitalhistory.uh.edu/learning_history/japanese_internment/newspaper_headlines.cfm (accessed 12 June 2009).

p. 40, "They were my best students.": quoted in William J. Cook, "May 2008—Manzanar War Relocation Center, CA," Weider History Group, www.historynet.com/manzanar.htm (accessed 21 May 2009).

p. 40, "These are law-abiding . . .": quoted in Ellen Eisenberg, "As Truly American as Your Son" (accessed 5 May 2009).

p. 40, "For the first time . . .": "S.F. Clear of All But 6 Sick Japs," *San Francisco Chronicle*, 21 May 1942, Virtual

Museum of the City of San Francisco, www.sfmuseum. net/shist8/evac19.html (accessed 7 May 2009).

p. 41, "The first sight . . .": Estelle Ishigo, *Lone Heart Mountain*, p. 6, University of California Libraries, http://content. cdlib.org/ark:/13030/hb6290111f/?order=8&brand=calis phere (accessed 21 May 2009).

p. 42, "According to journalism historian . . . blunder." Brian Thornton, "Heroic Editors in Short Supply During Japanese Internment," *Newspaper Research Journal*, Spring 2002, vol. 23, no. 2/3, pp. 99–113. http://web.ebscohost. com (accessed 17 November 2009).

p. 44, "At the racetracks . . . for each family.": *Confinement and Ethnicity*, p. 35.

p. 48, "More than 11,000 . . . as well.": Karen El Ebel, "WWII Violations of German American Civil Liberties by the US Government," *The Freedom of Information Times*, www.foitimes.com/internment/gasummary.htm (accessed 8 June 2009).

p. 48, ". . . more than 4,000 Germans . . . Jews.": Joseph E. Fallon, "History of the Internment of German American Civilians in the United States," *The Freedom of Information Times*, www.foitimes.com/internment/history.htm (accessed 8 June 2009).

p. 52, "About four thousand . . .": Jack Sutters, "American Refugees: The Japanese American Relocation," American Friends Service Committee, 2002, www.afsc.org/ht/d/ sp/i/16080/pid/16080 (accessed 25 May 2009).

p. 53, "I knew . . . wanted to serve.": Paul Tsuneishi, *Conscience and the Constitution*, Public Broadcasting

System, www.pbs.org/itvs/conscience/compliance/the_
draft/index.html (accessed 11 August 2009).

p. 54, "We don't . . . they're Japanese.": quoted in R. Douglas
Hurt, *The Great Plains during World War II* (Lincoln:
University of Nebraska Press, 2008), pp. 297–298.

p. 54, "the visiting . . . absolute minimum.": quoted in *The History
of the Heart Mountain Relocation Center*, www.heartmountain.
us/history.htm (accessed 11 August 2009).

p. 54, "I didn't know . . . they were content.": quoted in
Erin Kromm Cain, "Rohwer," University of Arkansas,
Research Frontiers, Spring 2009, http://researchfrontiers.
uark.edu/6283.php (accessed 11 August 2009).

Chapter Four

p. 56, "I could not . . . nothing had happened.": Frank Emi,
quoted in *Conscience and the Constitution*, Public Broadcasting
System, www.pbs.org/itvs/conscience/resistance/we_hereby
_refuse/index.html (accessed 11 August 2009).

p. 56, "We frankly . . . adopted country.": "Our Cards on the
Table," *Heart Mountain Sentinel*, March 11, 1944, quoted in
Conscience and the Constitution, Public Broadcasting System,
www.pbs.org/itvs/conscience/resistance/crackdown/05_
cards01_t.html (accessed 11 August 2009).

p. 57, "27. Are you willing . . . or organization.": "Statement
of United States Citizen of Japanese Ancestry," 1943,
quoted in *In Time & Place: Japanese Internment,* "The
Loyalty Questionnaire," www.intimeandplace.org/Japanese
%20Internment/reading/loyaltyquestions.html (accessed
8 June 2009).

p. 59, "The thing that struck me . . .": "Minoru Yasui," Human and Constitutional Rights, Columbia University Law School, 2008, www.hrcr.org/ccr/yasui.html (accessed 9 June 2009).

p. 60, "merely confuses the issue.": *Toyosaburo Korematsu v. United States,* 323 U.S. 214 (1944), http://caselaw.lp.findlaw.com/scripts/getcase.pl?court=US&vol=323&invol=214 (accessed 9 June 2009).

p. 61, "This exclusion . . . of racism.": *Toyosaburo Korematsu v. United States,* 323 U.S. 214 (1944).

p. 62, "Loyalty is . . . War Relocation Authority.": *Ex parte Mitsuye Endo,* 323 U.S. 283 (1944), http://caselaw.findlaw.com/cgi-bin/getcase.pl?court=us&vol=323&invol=283 (accessed 10 June 2009).

Chapter Five

p. 65, "Only about one-fourth . . .": *Personal Justice Denied,* p. 241.

p. 65, "We couldn't pack up . . .": "Paul Shinoda: 'volunteer' evacuee, Grand Junction, Colorado," quoted in *And Justice for All,* p. 55.

p. 67, ". . . the causes of the internment . . .": *Personal Justice Denied,* p. 18.

p. 68, "Executive Order 9066 . . . during World War II," *Personal Justice Denied,* p. 18.

p. 69, "The major problem . . .": Testimony of Dr. Ken Masugi, *Hearing before the Subcommittee on Administrative Practice and Procedure of the Committee on the Judiciary,* United States Senate, 27 July 1983, pp. 361, 363, *Internment*

Archives, www.internmentarchives.com/showdoc.php?doc id=00205&search_id=41216 (accessed 11 June 2009).

p. 69, "Of course the relocation . . .": Testimony of Senator S. I. Hayakawa, *Hearing before the Subcommittee,* p. 419, *Internment Archives,* www.internmentarchives.com/show doc.php?docid=00206&search_id=40479 (accessed 11 June 2009).

p. 72, "In my mind, . . . in those camps.": Tak Tsutsui, "Delegate Tak Tsutsui explains why he voted against apology," *Conscience and the Constitution,* Public Broadcasting System, www.pbs.org/itvs/conscience/who_writes_history /apology/index.html (accessed 11 August 2009).

p. 73, "[Korematsu] had his conviction . . .": "Remarks by the President at Medals of Freedom Presentation," Independent Living Research Utilization, 1998, www. ilru.org/html/about/Dart/President.html (accessed 11 June 2009).

p. 74, "Fred Korematsu challenged . . .": Asian American Bar Association, www.aaba-bay.com/aaba/showpage. asp?code=korematsucase (accessed 11 June 2009).

Chapter Six

p. 75, "Those who cannot remember . . .": "Ask the Editors: Frequently Asked Questions," *The Santayana Edition,* www.iupui.edu/~santedit/askedition.html (accessed 4 June 2009).

p. 75, ". . . Rehnquist . . . war is over.": William H. Rehnquist, "Remarks of Chief Justice William H. Rehnquist, 100th Anniversary Celebration of the Norfolk and Portsmouth

Bar Association, Norfolk, Virginia, May 3, 2000," www.
supremecourtus.gov/publicinfo/speeches/sp_05-03-00.
html (accessed 4 June 2009).

p. 76, "Grave injustices . . .": William Orville Douglas, *The
Court Years, 1939–1975: The Autobiography of William O.
Douglas* (New York: Random House, 1980), p. 280.

p. 76, "I have since . . . conscience-stricken.": "Biography: Earl
Warren." www.spartacus.schoolnet.co.uk/JFKwarren.
htm (accessed 4 June 2009).

p. 77, "I can't sleep . . . get out of it.": quoted in Dillon S.
Myer, *An Autobiography of Dillon S. Myer: Oral History
Transcript* (Berkeley: University of California Bancroft
Library, 1970), pp. 183–184, www.archive.org/stream/
autobiodillon00myerrich/autobiodillon00myerrich_
djvu.txt (accessed 4 June 2009).

p. 77, ". . . an inhuman mistake.": quoted in *Personal Justice
Denied*, p. 401.

p. 79, "In a December 2004 . . . some way.": Erik C. Nisbet
and James Shanahan, *MSRG Special Report: Restrictions
on Civil Liberties, Views of Islam, & Muslim Americans*,
December 2004, Table 7. Public Support for Restrictions
on Muslim Americans.

p. 79, "by allowing . . . of the past.": Brief *Amicus Curiae*
of Fred Korematsu . . ., *Donald Rumsfeld v. Jose Padilla*,
April 2004, http://supreme.lp.findlaw.com/supreme_
court/briefs/03-1027/03-1027.mer.ami.korematsu.pdf
(accessed 11 June 2009).

p. 79, "The extreme nature . . . military necessity.": Brief of
Amicus Curiae Fred Korematsu in Support of Petitioners,

Khaled F .A. Al Odah et al v. United States of America, Shafiq Rasul, et al. v. George W. Bush, et al., and *Yasir Esam Hamdi v. Donald Rumsfeld,* 2003, www.equaljusticesociety.org/ Korematsu_amicus_brief.pdf (accessed 11 June 2009).

p. 80, "Preserving our freedom . . . trial or hearing.": "Statement of U.S. Senator Russ Feingold on the Anti-Terrorism Bill," http://ispu.org/files/PDFs/cornell report. pdf, p. 6 (accessed 17 November 2009).

p. 81, "[The act] creates . . . during emergencies.": John Yoo and Eric Posner, "The Patriot Act under Fire," American Enterprise Institute for Public Policy, 1 December 2003, www.aei.org/issue/19661 (accessed 11 June 2009).

p. 83, "May [this memorial] serve . . .": *Poston, Arizona,* Japanese American Veterans Association, www.javadc. org/poston.htm (accessed 12 June 2009).

Further Information

Books

Burgan, Michael. *The Japanese American Internment: Civil Liberties Denied*. Minneapolis, MN: Compass Point Books, 2007.

Donlan, Leni. *How Did This Happen Here? Japanese Internment Camps* (American History Through Primary Sources). Chicago: Raintree, 2007.

Gold, Susan Dudley. *Korematsu v. United States: Japanese American Internment*. New York: Marshall Cavendish Benchmark, 2006.

Hanel, Rachael. *The Japanese American Internment: An Interactive History Adventure*. Mankato, MN: Capstone Press, 2008.

Kent, Deborah. *The Tragic History of the Japanese American Internment Camps*. Berkeley Heights, NJ: Enslow, 2008.

Sakuri, Gail. *Japanese American Internment Camps*. Danbury, CT: Children's Press, 2007.

Stewart, Todd (photographer); Natasha Egan, Karen J. Leong, and John Tateishi (contributors). *Placing Memory: A Photographic Exploration of Japanese American Internment*. Norman: University of Oklahoma Press, 2008.

Tashiro, Kenneth. *"Wase Time!": A Teen's Memoir of Gila River Internment Camp*. Bloomington, IN: AuthorHouse, 2005.

DVDs

Most Honorable Son. 60 minutes. PBS Home Video, 2007.

Time of Fear. 60 minutes. PBS Home Video, 2005.

Unfinished Business: The Japanese American Internment Cases. 58 minutes. New Video Group, 2005.

Victims of Circumstance. 120 minutes. Kawayan Productions, 2006.

Websites

Children of the Camps: Internment History
www.children-of-the-camps.org/history/index.html
This site focuses on the experiences of interned children, along with a timeline and camp description.

Densho: The Japanese American Legacy Project
www.densho.org/
Features lessons, photos, and video interviews with hundreds of Japanese Americans who survived the internment.

Digital History — Explorations: Japanese American Internment
www.digitalhistory.uh.edu/learning_history/japanese_internment/internment_decision.cfm
A study of the internment through primary source documents, videos, photographs, and other media.

Evacuation and Internment of San Francisco Japanese
www.sfmuseum.net/war/evactxt.html
A survey of internment events in the San Francisco area through newspaper accounts of the time.

A More Perfect Union: Japanese Americans and the U.S. Constitution

americanhistory.si.edu/perfectunion/non-flash/overview.html

An exploration of events before, during, and after the internment in light of constitutional issues.

Organizations and Places to Visit

Manzanar National Historic Site
P.O. Box 426
5001 Highway 395
Independence, CA 93526
760-878-2194
www.nps.gov/manz/

Japanese American Citizens League
1765 Sutter Street
San Francisco, CA 94115
415-921-5225
www.jacl.org/

Japanese American National Museum
369 East First Street
Los Angeles, CA 90012
213-625-0414
www.janm.org/

Bibliography

Books

Burton, Jeffery, Mary M. Farrell, Eleanor Roosevelt, Florence B. Lord, and Irene J. Cohen. *Confinement and Ethnicity: An Overview of World War II Japanese American Relocation Sites.* Seattle: University of Washington Press, 2002.

Daniels, Roger. *Asian America: Chinese and Japanese in the United States since 1850.* Seattle: University of Washington Press, 1990.

Daniels, Roger, Sandra C. Taylor, and Harry H. L. Kitano, eds. *Japanese Americans, from Relocation to Redress.* Rev. ed. Seattle: University of Washington Press, 1991.

Dollinger, Marc. *Quest for Inclusion.* Princeton, NJ: Princeton University Press, 2000.

Douglas, William Orville. *The Court Years, 1939–1975: The Autobiography of William O. Douglas.* New York: Random House, 1980.

Gesensway, Deborah, and Mindy Roseman. *Beyond Words: Images from America's Concentration Camps.* Ithaca, NY: Cornell University Press, 1987.

Katshima, Tetsuden. *Judgment without Trial: Japanese American Imprisonment during World War II.* Seattle: University of Washington Press, 2004.

Takezawa, Yasuko I. *Breaking the Silence: Redress and Japanese American Ethnicity.* Ithaca, NY: Cornell University Press, 1995.

Tateishi, John. *And Justice for All: An Oral History of the Japanese American Detention Camps.* Seattle: University of Washington Press, 1999.

Toshio Yatsushiro, "The Japanese Americans," in *American Minorities: A Textbook of Readings in Intergroup Relations,* ed. Milton L. Barron (New York: Knopf, 1957), page 319.

United States Commission on Wartime Relocation and Internment of Civilians. *Personal Justice Denied.* Seattle: University of Washington Press, 1997.

Websites

Civil Liberties Public Education Fund. "CLPEF Resolution Regarding Terminology." http://www.momomedia.com/CLPEF/backgrnd.html#Link%20to%20terminology (accessed 9 October 2009).

Eisenberg, Ellen. "As Truly American as Your Son: Voicing Opposition to Internment in Three West Coast Cities." *Oregon Historical Quarterly,* 22 December 2003. http://www.historycooperative.org/journals/ohq/104.4/eisenberg.html (accessed 5 May 2009).

Executive Order 9066. http://www.ourdocuments.gov/doc.php?doc=74 (accessed 4 May 2009).

"Franklin D. Roosevelt's 'Day of Infamy' Speech." http://www.ibiblio.org/hyperwar/PTO/EastWind/Infamy.html (accessed 3 May 2009).

Freedom of Information Times. http://www.foitimes.com/internment/ (accessed 8 June 2009).

In Time & Place: Japanese Internment. http://www.intime and place.org/Japanese%20Internment/index.html (accessed 8 June 2009).

Institute for Leadership Development and Study of Pacific and Asian North American Religion. "Gloria Morita on the Manzanar Internment." http://www.panainstitute.org/nisei-gloria-morita-manzanar-eo-9066 (accessed 7 May 2009).

Internment Archives. http://www.internmentarchives.com/index.php (accessed 11 June 2009).

Ishigo, Estelle. *Lone Heart Mountain.* University of California Libraries. http://content.cdlib.org/ark:/13030/hb6290111f/?order=8&brand=calisphere (accessed 21 May 2009).

Krebs, A. V. "Banishment from the 'Gold Mountain'." *Agriculture and Human Values* 12, no. 3 (June 1995). http://www.springerlink.com/index/P087580542P40164.pdf (accessed 5 May 2009).

Masaoka, Mike. "The Japanese American Creed." http://www.javoice.com/masaoka.html (accessed 26 May 2009).

Mintz, S. "Explorations: Japanese American Internment," *Digital History,* 2007,

http://www.digitalhistory.uh.edu/learning_history/japanese_internment/internment_decision.cfm (accessed 12 June 2009).

Myer, Dillon S. *An Autobiography of Dillon S. Myer: Oral History Transcript.* Berkeley: University of California Bancroft Library, 1970. http://www.archive.org/stream/ autobiodillon00myerrich/autobiodillon00myerrich_djvu.txt (accessed 4 June 2009).

National Archives and Records Administration. http://www. archives.gov/ (accessed 10 June 2009).

Time, "Rumbles from the Coast," 23 February 1942. http:// www.time.com/time/magazine/article/0,9171,884436,00. html?promoid=googlep (accessed 5 May 2009).

University of Denver. *Behind Barbed Wire at Amache.* http:// www.du.edu/behindbarbedwire/ (accessed 4 May 2009).

University of Washington Libraries. "Interrupted Lives: Can't Believe It's True—Pearl Harbor." http://www.lib. washington.edu/exhibits/harmony/UW-new/one/ (accessed 5 May 2009).

U.S. Supreme Court. Brief *Amicus Curiae* of Fred Korematsu . . . *Donald Rumsfeld v. Jose Padilla,* April 2004. http://supreme. lp.findlaw.com/supreme_court/briefs/03-1027/03-1027.mer. ami.korematsu.pdf (accessed 11 June 2009).

———. Brief of *Amicus Curiae* Fred Korematsu in Support of Petitioners. *Khaled F. A. Al Odah et al v. United States of America, Shafiq Rasul, et al. v. George W. Bush, et al.*, and *Yasir Esam Hamdi v. Donald Rumsfeld,* 2003. http://www.equaljusticesociety.org/ Korematsu_amicus_brief.pdf (accessed 11 June 2009).

———. *Ex parte Mitsuye Endo,* 323 U.S. 283 (1944). http://caselaw.findlaw.com/cgi-bin/getcase.pl?court= us&vol=323&invol=283 (accessed 10 June 2009).

———. *Toyosaburo Korematsu v. United States,* 323 U.S. 214 (1944). http://laws.findlaw.com/us/323/214.html (accessed 5 May 2009).

Virtual Museum of the City of San Francisco. "Internment of San Francisco Japanese." http://www.sfmuseum.net/war/ evactxt.html (accessed 7 May 2009).

Yu, C. John. *The Japanese American Internment.* http://www. geocities.com/Athens/8420/main.html (accessed 26 May 2009).

Index

Page numbers in **boldface** are illustrations.

evacuation. *See* detention.
Executive Order 9066, 32, 34, 66, 68

farming, 9, **10**, 11, 12, 28–29, 30, 38, 39, 47, 52, 54, 65
Federal Bureau of Investigation (FBI), 17, 26, 27, 29
Ford, Gerald, 66

Gentlemen's Agreement, 11
Gould, Rosalie, 54
Granada internment camp. *See* Amache internment camp.

Hayakawa, S. I., 69–70
Heart Mountain internment camp, 47, 54, 56, 73
Hirabayashi, Gordon, 58–59, **61**, 70
Hoover, J. Edgar, 29

Immigration Act (1924), 12
Ishigo, Estelle, 41
Issei, 12, 14, 17, 23, 25, 26, 27, 29, 37, 55, 56

Japan, 6, 11, 14–**15**, 16, 19, 28, 64
Japanese American Citizens League (JACL), 22, 24, 26, 55, 56, 58, 66, 67, 72, 73
Japanese American Creed, 22, 24–25, 73

Kibei, 55–56
Korematsu, Fred, 60–**61**, 62, 70, 73–74, 76, 79

Lippmann, Walter, 28

Manzanar internment camp, 45, **46**, **51**, 58, 73, **74**

About the Author

ANN HEINRICHS is the award-winning author of more than two hundred books on U.S. and world history, geography, culture, and political affairs. Other books include science and nature, biography, and English grammar topics. She has also worked as a children's book editor and an advertising copywriter. World exploration is her passion, and she has traveled through Africa, the Middle East, Europe, and East Asia. Heinrichs lives in Chicago, Illinois, where she enjoys bicycling and kayaking.